Studying God's Word

Book B

A Study of the Doctrines of the Christian Faith

Michael J. McHugh

Christian Liberty Press

Arlington Heights, Illinois

This book is based on the *Catechism for Young Children*,
written by Joseph P. Engels in the 1840s.

Printing 2013

A publication of

Christian Liberty Press

502 West Euclid Avenue

Arlington Heights, Illinois 60004

www.christianlibertypress.com

Written and compiled by Michael J. McHugh

Typesetting by Lina King

Layout and graphics by Eric D. Bristley

Special thanks goes to Raymond and Renee Monroe for permission to use material and ideas from their writings and for editorial assistance.

Appreciation is also due to Great Commission Publications for the use and adaptation of the *Catechism for Young Children: An Introduction to the Shorter Catechism*.

ISBN 978-1-930092-57-0

    1-930092-57-1

Printed in the United States of America

Table of Contents

Preface

One of the primary goals of the **Studying God's Word** series is to encourage students to conform their thinking to the standard of God's revealed Word. When students begin to bring every thought into captivity to God's Word, they begin to realize the joy of being conformed to the image of Jesus Christ.

In this workbook, an emphasis is placed on the need for young people to develop an understanding of basic Bible doctrine. Students are not only presented with important facts and truths from the Bible; they are also provided with a wealth of personal examples from the lives of God's people that illustrate the truths they need to comprehend. **Studying God's Word Book B** also contains helpful Catechism drill and memory work.

Starting with **Studying God's Word Book E**, this series uses a chronological approach to Bible study so young people can understand the timing and order of the key events listed throughout the Bible. This approach permits students to gain an accurate understanding of the flow of events contained in the Bible.

It has often been said that these are the times that try men's souls. Modern American culture is confronting God's people, both young and old alike, with many challenging trials and temptations. More than ever before, young people need to be equipped with the whole armor of God's Word so they can withstand the fiery darts of the wicked one. May the Lord use this Bible study workbook to equip His children with the spiritual weapons that they need to fight the good fight of faith.

Michael J. McHugh

Arlington Heights, Illinois

1995

Acknowledgments

The author would like to give credit to various individuals for contributing to the successful completion of this Bible Study workbook.

First and foremost, I would like to thank Raymond and Renee Monroe for granting me permission to use material and ideas from their own writings as well as for their editorial assistance.

Grateful appreciation is also extended to Joyce M. Horton for her helpful book on how to teach the catechism to children. This work helped me to focus the book in an orderly direction.

Thanks are also extended to Great Commission Publications for the use and adaptation of the *Catechism for Young Children*, originally written by Joseph P. Engels in the 1840s.

Finally, I would like to thank Lina King and Eric Bristley for their assistance in typesetting and designing the graphics for this workbook. Without the help of these individuals, and ultimately of God himself, this project would never have been completed.

How To Use This Book

The basic approach presented in this workbook is simple. Each Unit is broken up into five separate lessons. Most educators will take one week to complete each Unit by doing one lesson each day from Monday through Friday.

Sunday school teachers who use this material may wish to modify the above listed schedule by doing the first two lessons in each unit on one Sunday with the goal of completing lesson three through five the next Lord's Day. These suggestions are always subject to change and instructors are encouraged to develop a schedule that works well for their particular teaching situation.

It should also be stressed that this workbook is designed to be taught to children, ages 6-8, who are often incapable of completing Bible study activities on an independent basis. Therefore, instructors must plan on working through each lesson with their students.

In this regard, not all young children have the same level of ability in areas such as memorization and the completion of projects. Consequently, teachers must be ready and willing to accept the fact that some of their children may not be able to successfully complete every memory project or activity in their workbook. Simply encourage each of your students to do the best they can with each lesson or activity.

The Catechism Drill activities present many of the doctrines of the Christian faith to young minds. Some of the doctrines taught in the Bible are not easy to explain or to totally comprehend. Therefore, instructors should not become discouraged if their students do not grasp each and every Bible doctrine presented in the Catechism itself or in the Bible in general. Most children need to have the key teachings of the Christian faith presented several times over a period of years before they finally sink deep into their minds and hearts. The goal of this workbook is to present children with a foundation for understanding the Bible, the way of salvation, and the Christian life. The truths that your students do learn will need to be nurtured and expanded upon over a long season of time. Never lose sight of the fact that you are beginning to guide children into the truth.

This workbook is focused around a total of sixty Catechism questions. Special review units are provided at the end of every set of twenty questions to help you insure that your students are retaining the catechism information. We encourage teachers to use the award certificates that are printed in the back of this workbook as their students successfully complete their memory work.

Finally, we recommend that instructors purchase a supplemental cassette tape and song book that is designed to re-enforce the Catechism questions. This tape and song book are entitled **Why Can't I See God?** by Judy Rogers. Individuals may order this excellent musical supplement by contacting:

Presbyterian and Reformed Publishing Co.
P.O. Box 817 (*mailing address*)
1102 Marble Hill Road (*shipping address*)
Phillipsburg, NJ 08865-0817

Telephone # 1-800-631-0094

May the Lord bless you as you teach children the precious truths of the Christian faith.

Thy word is a lamp unto my feet,
and a light unto my path.
— Psalm 119:105

The earth is the Lord's,
and the fulness thereof;
the world,
and they that dwell therein.
— Psalm 24:1

Unit 1   God Made Me

Catechism Drill

1. Question: Who made you?
   Answer: **God made me.**

2. Question: What else did God make?
   Answer: **God made all things.**

3. Question: Why did God make you and everything else?
   Answer: **God made all things for His own glory.**

Catechism Drill was memorized on _____ (date).

Scripture Reading

Read Genesis Chapter One and discuss the six days of creation with your teacher.

Words you need to know from the Bible

Create	To make something out of nothing (only God can do this)
Fruitful	To grow and multiply in number
Dominion	To rule over something or someone
Image	A physical or spiritual likeness of someone or something
Divided	To put things into separate parts

1

Lesson 3

Bible Story

Read the story of John the Baptist's birth in Luke 1:39-80. This story teaches that God creates each person. Adam and Eve were simply the first people God made. Each person God makes has a special purpose in His plan. Note Ecclesiastes 3:1-2. This passage teaches that God sends people into the world at the right time in history to carry out His plans.

Lesson 4

Written Exercise

Complete the sentences using the words below.

glory	made	animals	Genesis

1. We learn about how God made the world and all things by reading the book of _____.

2. God _____ Adam and Eve.

3. In six days, God made all things for his own _____.

4. All _____ were made by God.

Activity

Lesson 5

Place a photograph of yourself in this space or draw a picture of your-self.

My name is _____.   God made me in my
                        (Your name)

mother's womb before I was born on _____ (date).
                                              (Birthdate)

Extra Activity

With your teacher's help, make a banner depicting the six days of the Creation week.

Unit 2   I Should Glorify God

Catechism Drill

4.   Question: How can you glorify God?

     Answer: By loving Him and
doing what He commands.

5.   Question: Why should you glorify God?

     Answer: Because He made me
and takes care of me.

Catechism Drill was memorized on _____ (date).

Scripture Reading

Read 1 John 5:1-3 and Matthew 22:35-40. These Bible passages teach us that we can do good works only if they are done in harmony with God's Word, out of a heart of faith, for the glory of God. Our works can never save our souls. Only by believing in Christ's work on the cross can we receive salvation. We can glorify our Creator with true good works only when our hearts are cleansed by faith. Close this lesson by reading Ecclesiastes 12:13-14.

Words you need to know from the Bible

Glorify	To praise and honor someone
Commandments	God's rules for life and living
Love	Serving another out of respect and devotion
Grievous	difficult or painful

Lesson 3

Bible Story

Read the story of the Good Samaritan from Luke 10:25-37. Talk about the various people in the story with your teacher to determine who brought glory to God through his actions. Read Matthew 5:16 and discuss why a Christian has the duty to let his light shine before other people.

Lesson 4

Written Exercise

Complete the sentences by using the words below.

light	God	commands	glorify

1. We can glorify God by doing what He _____.

2. Jesus said, "Let your _____ shine before men…"

3. We should _____ God because he made us and cares for us.

4. Only _____ deserves to receive glory and honor.

Lesson 5

Activity

With your teacher's help, make up a play based upon the story of the Good Samaritan. Each member of your family or class should choose a character from the story and take responsibility for preparing his costume. It may be helpful for your teacher to give the actors written cards with their lines on it and plenty of "walk through" practice. Close the play by reading James 4:17 out loud with the actors.

Unit 3   God is a Trinity

Catechism Drill

6.   Question: Are there more gods than one?

    Answer: There is only one God.

7.   Question: How many persons are this one true God?

    Answer: Three persons.

8.   Question: Who are they?

    Answer: The Father, the Son, and the Holy Spirit.

Catechism Drill was memorized on _____ (date).

Scripture Reading

Read Deuteronomy 6:4-5 and Mark 12:28-34. These Bible passages help us to understand the biblical teaching that there is only one God. In addition, read 1 John 5:4-7 and Matthew 28:16-20 to understand more about God. Talk about the nature of God with your teacher. Remember, the true God is one God in three special persons.

Words you need to know from the Bible

Godhead	One God that exists in a perfect union of three persons or trinity
Father	God the Father, the first person of the Trinity
Son	God the Son, the second person of the Trinity
Holy Spirit	God the Holy Spirit, the third person of the Trinity

Bible Story

Lesson 3

Read the story of Elijah on Mount Carmel from 1 Kings 18:17-39. This Bible passage will help you to understand that there is only one true and living God.

In addition, read the story from Matthew 3:13-17 regarding the baptism of Jesus. This story will help you see all three members of the Trinity are active at the same time. This story is a powerful witness to the truth that God exists as one being in three persons.

Written Exercise

Lesson 4

Complete the sentences using the words below.

Son	three	Godhead	Elijah

1. The true God is one God in _____ persons.

2. Jesus Christ is the _____ of God.

3. The _____ is Father, Son, and Holy Spirit.

4. _____ showed the people of Israel that there was only one true and living God.

Lesson 5

Activity

You have just learned that the Bible teaches that the Godhead (Father, Son, and Holy Spirit) is one God in three persons. This truth is too hard for us to totally understand. We must accept this teaching by faith.

The activity that follows will help you to better understand how the Trinity is reflected in creation. The Bible often refers to God as Light because He lights up our sin-darkened world. But, have you ever looked closely at the sunlight that shines upon you?

Ask your teacher or parent to help you find a special piece of glass known as a "prism." If you hold this prism up in the air, so the sunlight shines upon it, you will see that the one light of the sun gives off many different shades of light. There are three main colors that make up white light; blue, red and green. This reminds us of the Trinity—one God in three persons!

This wonderful show of lights helps us to see another way in which God is like light. He is one God, but He shines as three great persons when He shines upon the world with His love.

Unit 4   God is a Spirit

Catechism Drill

9.   Question: What is God?

   Answer: God is a Spirit,
   and has not a body like men.

Catechism Drill was memorized on _____ (date).

Scripture Reading

Read John 4:24 and Acts 17:22-25, discuss the subject of God as a Spirit with your teacher.

Words you need to know from the Bible

Spirit   A person who thinks, feels, wills, knows, acts, but has no physical human body

Body   A physical body with flesh and blood that we can see and touch

Lord   Supreme Ruler or Divine Being

Bible Story

Read the story of the apostle Paul on Mars' Hill from Acts 17:22-34. This story teaches us that the Lord God, the Creator of the earth, is not to be worshipped in images made by men. We must worship God through the Holy Spirit by faith in a manner that is true to God's Word.

Lesson 4

Written Exercise

Complete the sentences by using the words below.

Spirit	Holy	Mars'	body

1. We must worship God in _____ and in truth.

2. God does not have a _____ as we do.

3. We must worship God through the _____ Spirit.

4. The Apostle Paul spoke on _____ Hill.

Lesson 5

Activity

Make a clay tablet shaped like the picture shown below with your teacher's help. Glue a piece of paper to the front of the tablet with the Second Commandment written on it. Ask your teacher to help you print the Second Commandment.

Thou shalt not make unto thee any graven image, or any likeness of anything that is in heaven above, or that is in the earth beneath, or that is in the water under the earth: Thou shalt not bow down thyself to them, nor serve them

Unit 5   God is Everywhere

Lesson 1

Catechism Drill

10. Question: Where is God?

       Answer: God is everywhere.

Catechism Drill was memorized on _____ (date).

Lesson 2

Scripture Reading

Read Psalm 139:1-10 and Acts 17:24-28. These Bible verses teach us that the Spirit of the Lord is present in every part of His creation. God always sees what is happening in the world. Nothing in this world ever takes God by surprise for He is everywhere at the same time.

Words you need to know from the Bible

Everywhere	In every place at the same time
Flee	To run away from someone or something
Presence	When someone is with others or is in a place
Ascend	To go up

Lesson 3

Bible Story

Read the story of the Prophet Jonah from Jonah Chapter One and Two. This Bible story teaches us that it is foolish to try to hide from God. It also teaches us the wonderful truth that God can help us and care for us wherever we go in this wide world. As Acts Chapter 17 teaches, God is not very far from any person. All people who truly seek after God will find him.

Lesson 4

Written Exercise

Complete the sentences using the words below.

seek	hide	God	everywhere

1. No person is able to _____ from God.

2. God is _____ at the same time.

3. _____ is not very far from any person.

4. All people who _____ God will find Him.

Lesson 5

Activity

Color this picture of Jonah and the whale.

Unit 6   God is Invisible

Catechism Drill

11. Question: Can you see God?

    Answer: No, I cannot see God,
    but he can always see me.

Catechism Drill was memorized on _____ (date).

Scripture Reading

Read John 1:18 and 1 Timothy 1:17. These verses teach us that God is invisible. Also, read Proverbs 15:3 and Hebrews 4:12-13. These Bible passages teach us that God can **always** see us. God never sleeps or takes a nap. God is so big that His Spirit cannot be bound by a human body or the sky above us. The Lord is everywhere.

Words you need to know from the Bible

Invisible	A real thing or person that cannot be seen
Always	Something that happens over and over and will never change
Eternal	There is no beginning nor end to God

Bible Story

Read the story about the Prophet Elijah speaking to the invisible God from 1 Kings 19:1-18. This story helps us to see that God is so powerful that He can control winds, earthquakes, and fire without using a physical body. God does not need a body to do what He wants. The mighty Lord, our Creator, can make things happen by simply commanding something to happen.

Lesson 4

Written Exercise

Complete the sentences using the words below.

always	invisible	sleep	voice

1. We cannot see God because He is _____ .

2. God can _____ see us.

3. The Lord never gets tired or goes to _____ .

4. God spoke to Elijah in a still small _____ .

Lesson 5

Activity

Color the shapes with dots in them to discover a hidden picture. Let this activity be a reminder of the fact that nothing can be hidden from God.

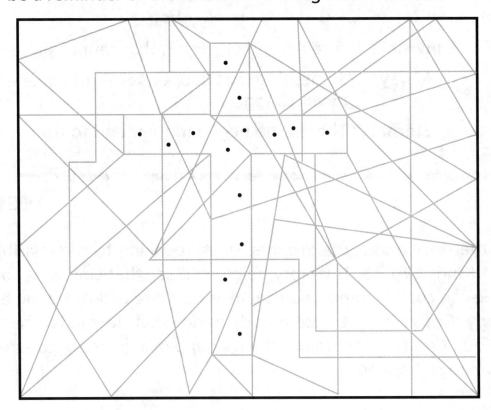

Unit 7   God Sees Me

Catechism Drill

12. Question: Does God know everything?

   Answer: Yes, nothing can be hidden
          from God.

Catechism Drill was memorized on _____ (date).

Lesson 2

Scripture Reading

Read 1 John 3:18-20 and Luke 16:13-15. These Bible passages help us to understand that God knows everything. Matthew Chapter Ten tells us that God knows even the number of hairs on our head! He also knows when a little sparrow falls to the ground because God is concerned about caring for everything He has made. Have your teacher read the story of Achan from Joshua Chapter Seven to help remind you of the foolishness of trying to hide things from God.

Words you need to know from the Bible

Hidden   To keep something from being seen by another

Knoweth   To have good understanding

Nothing   Nothing of any kind or amount

Lesson 3

Bible Story

Read the story of the Woman at the Well as recorded in John 4:1-42. This Bible story teaches us that God knows every tiny detail about our lives and about everything else that is going on in the world.

Written Exercises

Lesson 4

Complete the sentences using the words below.

hairs	everything	God	hide

1. Nothing can be hid from _____ .

2. God knows the number of _____ on your head.

3. Achan tried to _____ things from God.

4. Our great and mighty God knows _____ .

Activity

Lesson 5

Ask your teacher to help you organize a special activity known as a "treasure hunt." Start by getting six things from around the house such as a piece of candy or a small toy. Then, find a good hiding place for each item.

With your teacher's help, write up clues for those young people who will be trying to find the things that you hid around the house. You have to decide if you want to give these things away as prizes if they are found.

After your friends have found your hidden things, you may want to talk about the fact that God always knows where everything is placed. Help your friends to understand that although we can sometimes hide things from other people, we cannot hide things from God. The wisdom and power of God controls everything and everyone.

Unit 8   God Can Do Anything

Lesson 1

Catechism Drill

13. Question: Can God do all things?

     Answer: Yes, God can do all His holy will.

Catechism Drill was memorized on _____ (date).

Lesson 2

Scripture Reading

Read Philippians 2:5-13 and Job 42:1-2. These Bible verses help us to know that the Lord can do anything that He wants to at any time. It is important to remember that God never wants to do anything that is not holy and wise. Therefore, if God decides to do something, He always does what is good. It is impossible for God to do anything bad or sinful. The Lord is perfect in His holiness.

Words you need to know from the Bible

Impossible	Something that cannot be done
Holy	Pure and set apart for God's use
God's will	The things that God wants to do
Confess	To declare that something or someone is true

Lesson 3

Bible Story

Read the story of Joshua fighting the Amorites with God's strength and help from Joshua 10:6-15. This Bible story teaches us that God can do anything he wants, with or without the help of men. He made the sun stand still! The Lord's power is without limit and He can do all His holy will.

Lesson 4

Written Exercise

Complete the sentences using the words below.

impossible	holy	Amorites	Joshua

1. God can do all His _____ will.

2. Nothing is _____ with God.

3. God made the sun and moon stand still for _____ .

4. Joshua fought against the _____ with God's help.

Lesson 5

Activity

Color the picture of Joshua fighting against the Amorites.

Unit 9   The Bible is Our Rule

Catechism Drill

14. Question: Where do you learn how to love and obey God?

     Answer: In the Bible alone.

Catechism Drill was memorized on _____ (date).

Scripture Reading

Read 2 Timothy 3:15-17 and Matthew 4:1-4. These Bible passages help us to understand that only the Bible can give us the pure Word of God. Wise Christians will go directly to the Bible to find out exactly what God wants them to do to please Him. Thankfully, we do not have to rely upon the wisdom of men to tell us how to love and obey God. We can hear directly from God by reading His Word and thereby follow the guidance of the Holy Spirit.

Words you need to know from the Bible

Inspiration	God given words; as if God breathed the words out of His own mouth
Love	Serving another out of respect and devotion
Obey	To follow the rules or commands of another
Alone	By yourself; without anyone else
Rule	A guide or standard by which we can measure other things

Lesson 3

Bible Story

Read the story of the Bible students at Berea from Acts 17:1-12. This story helps us to see that God honors Bible students who always "test" everything that they are taught by seeing if it agrees with Holy Scripture. The Word of God called the Christians in Berea "noble" because they listened carefully to the missionary teachers and then compared what they heard with the Bible itself. We should follow the example of these noble and godly people as we study the Holy Scriptures. We should be quick to reject any teaching that does not measure up to the standards of God's Word. Close by reading Galatians 1:6-12 with your teacher and ask your teacher to explain this passage.

Lesson 4

Written Exercise

Complete the sentences using the words below.

noble	alone	quick	Bible

1. The _____ teaches us how to love and obey God.

2. Christians living in Berea were called _____ .

3. We must be _____ to reject any teaching that goes against the Bible.

4. The Bible _____ gives us the true Words of God.

Lesson 5

Activity

Ask your teacher to help you make a scroll with the directions that follow. During Bible times, most letters or books were put into a scroll.

Take three pieces of notebook paper and glue them together edge to edge. You should overlap each page about 1/4 of an inch so the pages can be glued together easily. Next, get two round sticks about twelve inches long and glue them onto the outside edges of the wide piece of paper. Roll the paper around each stick tightly until the two sticks meet in the middle of the paper.

After you have made the scroll, you can open it up and print your favorite Bible verse on the paper. Ask your teacher to help you with the printing if you are having trouble.

Thy _____ *is a* _____ *unto my* _____ *and a* _____ *unto my* _____.

—Psalm 119:105

Unit 10   The Bible is God's Word

Catechism Drill

15. Question: Who wrote the Bible?

    Answer: Prophets, who wrote by the
                 inspiration of the Holy Spirit.

Catechism Drill was memorized on _____ (date).

Scripture Reading

Read 2 Peter 1:16-21 and 2 Timothy 3:16-17. These Bible verses teach us that God chose faithful and dedicated men called prophets to write the Holy Scriptures. Each writer of Scripture wrote down exactly what the Holy Spirit wanted them to write. In this way the Bible is really God speaking to us. God chose these godly men to write down the special messages that He wanted to give to mankind. The Bible is made up of 66 small books.

Many of the books in the New Testament Scripture are really letters that were written to groups of Christians who lived during the time just after Jesus returned to heaven. These letters, written under the direction of the Holy Spirit, helped early believers to know how to live and work like Jesus.

Words you need to know from the Bible

Wrote	When someone writes down some words
Holy Scriptures	The Sixty-six books of the Bible
Prophecy	To speak or proclaim God's Words to others
Interpretation	To explain the words of another

22

Bible Story

Lesson 3

Read the story of Moses receiving the Words of God as a prophet in Exodus Chapter Twenty. This teaches us one way in which God chose to give holy men the words that they were to pass on to mankind. All Christians should understand the importance of learning to read and write well. God has chosen to use the written word to pass on His directions and rules for faith and life. Close this lesson by reading Romans 10:17.

Written Exercise

Lesson 4

Complete the sentences using the words below.

prophet	chose	sixty-six	inspired

1. God the Holy Spirit _____ each writer of Scripture.

2. God _____ and inspired each person who helped to write the Bible.

3. Moses was a _____ as he received and spoke God's Words.

4. The Bible is made up of _____ books.

Activity

Lesson 5

Make a felt banner with the names of the sixty-six books of the Bible pasted on it. Your teacher can help you cut out small pieces of paper and print the names of each book in the Bible on each piece. After you have glued each name on your banner in the correct order that they appear in the Bible, you can hang your banner in your bedroom.

Unit 11   Our First Parents

Catechism Drill

16. Question: Who were our first parents?

    Answer: Adam and Eve.

17. Question: How did God make our first parents?

    Answer: God made Adam's body out of the ground, and Eve's body out of a rib from Adam.

Catechism Drill was memorized on _____ (date).

Scripture Reading

Read Genesis 2:7-23 and Genesis 3:20. These Bible passages teach us that Adam and Eve were the first human beings created by God. It was God who decided to make Eve because He knew that it was not good for man to be alone. Adam and Eve were the first parents on earth. All of the families of earth can trace their beginning back to Adam and Eve. Read Acts 17:26 and Matthew 19:1-6 to see that all human beings descended from the first parents God made.

God made man out of the dust of the earth and formed woman out of man. The great Creator planned for men and women to become one flesh through the covenant of marriage. Men are not complete without women, and women are not complete without men. God wants Christian men and women, as well as Christian boys and girls, to work together in a spirit of Christian love. Christians can glorify their Creator in wonderful ways when they work together in a spirit of unity and brotherhood.

Words you need to know from the Bible

Parents	A man and woman who have children
Rib	A bone in the chest of a human body
Ground	The dust of the earth
Covenant	An agreement or promise between two or more persons

Lesson 3

Bible Story

Read the story of Adam and Eve from Genesis Chapter 1:26-31 and Genesis Chapter 2. This story teaches us that God made man in His own image to rule over the creatures He had made. God, in His wisdom, saw that man would need a helper if he was to do a good job in taking care of God's world. This is why God made Eve, so she could help her husband rule over the other creatures on the earth. It is important to remember that we still have the duty to take good care of God's world. But we can only do this the right way when we become servants of Jesus Christ.

Lesson 4

Written Exercise

Complete the sentences using the words below.

rib	dust	image	parents

1. Our first _____ were Adam and Eve.

2. Eve's body was made from the _____ of Adam.

3. God made man in His own _____ .

4. God made Adam's body out of the _____ of the ground.

Lesson 5

Activity

Color the picture of Adam and Eve that is shown below.

Unit 12 Our Spirits Never Die

Catechism Drill

18. Question: What did God give Adam and Eve besides bodies?

    Answer: He gave them spirits that will last forever.

19. Question: Do you have a spirit as well as a body?

    Answer: Yes, I have a spirit that can never die.

20. Question: How do you know your spirit will last forever?

    Answer: Because the Bible tells me so.

Catechism Drill was memorized on _____ (date).

Lesson 2

Scripture Reading

Read Genesis 2:7, 1 Corinthians 6:19-20, and Ecclesiastes 12:1-7. These verses from Scripture help us to understand that man was made differently from the animals. Animals do not have spirits. However, all people, beginning with Adam and Eve have been created with a spirit or soul by which they are aware of their duty to worship and obey God. All people are aware that God exists, that the world was created by God and that He made them. The Bible also calls this our conscience (Romans 2:15).

You have a physical body made up of flesh and blood. You also have a spiritual body or soul that God has put inside you. This body is not like your natural physical body, for it is invisible. Your soul will never cease to exist. God made your spirit so that it will last forever. Do you want to last forever in heaven or in hell?

27

Words you need to know from the Bible

Spirit	The invisible part of a human being that can worship God, also called the soul
Forever	Something that will never end even over time
Physical	The material visible part of man that includes flesh, bones, and blood
Gave	To have given someone something

Lesson 3

Bible Story

Read the story of Stephen being stoned from Acts 7:51-60. This Bible Story teaches us that people have spirits that live on after they die. In verse 59, Stephen prays that God would take hold of his spirit and bring it safely into the heavenly places. If we love God, the Lord Jesus will take our spirit or soul to live with Him in Heaven after our bodies die in the same manner as Stephen, the martyr. Close by reading 2 Corinthians 5:6-10.

Lesson 4

Written Exercises

Complete the sentences using the words below.

Stephen	spirits	physical	forever

1. Adam and Eve were given bodies and _____ .

2. All human beings have a spirit that will last _____ .

3. _____ asked God to receive his spirit.

4. The materials, flesh and blood, make up our _____ body.

Lesson 5

Activity

Color the picture of Stephen, the martyr, as he prays for those who are trying to kill him.

Unit 13   How God Made Us

Catechism Drill

21. Question: How good were Adam and Eve when God made them?

    Answer: **They were holy and happy.**

Catechism Drill was memorized on _____ (date).

Scripture Reading

Read Genesis 1:26-31 and Ephesians 4:17-24. These verses teach us that Adam and Eve were created by God to be holy and happy. In the beginning of the world, a Holy and righteous God made a man and a woman to be like Him.

Happiness is the result of being close to God and walking in His ways. If we do not obey God and walk in His ways, we can never be happy. Adam and Eve were only happy as long as they followed God's commandments. If you read Psalm 144:15, you will see that it says "…happy is that people, whose God is the Lord."

Words you need to know from the Bible

Holy	To be completely dedicated to God and separated from sin
Righteous	To act in a holy and obedient way toward God
Commandments	God's rules for human beings
Happy	To be filled with joy and gladness

Lesson 3

Bible Story

Read the story of Ezra leading the people back to God's Word and God's way from Nehemiah 8:1-10. This story helps us to see that the joy of the Lord is our strength. When people turn their hearts back to God, they have good reason to be happy. God desires for us to be holy <u>and</u> happy!

The Bible teaches us that it is God's desire that we glorify Him and enjoy Him forever. Close this lesson by reading Romans 14:17 with your teacher.

Lesson 4

Written Exercise

Complete the sentences using the words below.

happy	holy	Ezra	strength

1. God made Adam and Eve _____ and happy.

2. The joy of the Lord is our _____ .

3. A Holy God made Adam and Eve to be _____ .

4. The people became happy when _____ read God's Word.

Lesson 5

Activity

With your teacher's help, prepare and send a special card to someone you know who is sad. This project will help to get you in the habit of doing things to make other people happy. As a result, you will also be happy because you are following God's command to be kind. After you are done with your project, read Ephesians 4:32.

Unit 14   Catechism Review

Review catechism questions 1-21 with your teacher. Do your best to memorize each of these questions along with the proper answers. If you are able to answer all of the questions, you may ask your teacher to give you an Outstanding Achievement Award.

Catechism Review was successfully completed on _____(date).

Review Exercise (Catechism Questions 1-5)

Complete the sentences using the words below.

commands	glory	light	Genesis	God

1. In six days, God made all things for His own _____ .

2. The book of _____ teaches us how God made the world and all things.

3. We can glorify God by doing what He _____.

4. Jesus said, "Let your _____ shine before men."

5. Only _____ deserves to receive glory and honor.

Review Exercise (Catechism Questions 6-10)

Complete the sentences using the words below.

spirit	everywhere	Godhead	seek	hide

1. The _____ is Father, Son, and Holy Spirit.

2. We must worship God in _____ and in truth.

3. No person is able to _____ from God.

4. God is _____ at the same time.

5. All people who _____ God will find him.

Lesson 4

Review Exercise (Catechism Questions 11-15)

Complete the sentences using the words below.

sleep	Joshua	always	sixty-six	Bible

1. God can _____ see us.

2. The Lord never gets tired or goes to _____.

3. God made the sun and moon stand still for _____ .

4. The _____ teaches us how to love and obey God.

5. The Bible is made up of _____ books.

Lesson 5

Review Exercise (Catechism Questions 16-21)

Complete the sentences using the words below.

forever	physical	image	rib	holy

1. God made man in His own _____ .

2. All human beings have a spirit that will last _____ .

3. The materials, flesh and blood, make up our _____ body.

4. God made Adam and Eve _____ and happy.

5. Eve's body was made from the _____ of Adam.

Unit 15   Covenant Relationships

Catechism Drill

22. Question: What is a covenant?

    Answer: An agreement between
    two or more persons.

Catechism Drill was memorized on _____ (date).

Scripture Reading

Read Genesis 9:8-16. These Bible passages help us to understand what a covenant is all about. A covenant is an agreement or promise between two or more persons. Over the long years of history, the Lord has made many covenant promises with His chosen people.

For example, the Lord made a covenant promise with Noah. He promised Noah that He would never again destroy mankind with a flood. As a sign of this promise, God put a rainbow in the sky to remind each generation of His faithfulness. The Lord always keeps His Word. When God makes an agreement or a covenant with someone else, He always does what He promises.

Words you need to know from the Bible

Agreement	When two or more people make an arrangement
Promise	A pledge by someone to do something
Mankind	All human beings living on the earth
Nation	A whole country
Sacred	Something that is devoted to God and respected as holy

Lesson 3

Bible Story

Read the story of Abraham from Genesis 17:1-20 as he enters into a sacred covenant with God.

The Lord told Abraham that he would surely agree to bless him and his children for generations if they would faithfully walk in God's ways. This covenant was the beginning of the nation of Israel as a separate people who were called to follow God.

As it was true in the days of Abraham, so it is true today, blessed is the nation whose God is the Lord!

Lesson 4

Written Exercise

Complete the sentences using the words below.

promises	rainbow	covenant	Abraham

1. A _____ is an agreement between two or more people.

2. The Lord always does what He _____ .

3. God chose _____ to start a new nation called Israel.

4. The _____ is a sign of God's covenant with Noah.

Lesson 5

Activity

Color the picture of Noah's family and the Ark shown below.

Unit 16   The Covenant of Works

Catechism Drill

23. Question: What Covenant did God make with Adam?

    Answer: **The Covenant of works.**

24. Question: What did God require Adam to do in the covenant of works?

    Answer: **To obey Him perfectly.**

Catechism Drill was memorized on _____ (date).

Scripture Reading

Read Genesis 2:15-17. Shortly after man was created, God made an agreement with him. The man called Adam was required to do something in this covenant with God. Man was required to obey God perfectly and the Lord would in turn bless him as long as he obeyed.

It is very important for us to understand what God considers faithful obedience. True obedience does not mean that we obey God sometimes, or perhaps when we feel like it. The Bible teaches that God expects all people to do exactly what He requires in the way He requires it. And we must obey Him out of a cheerful heart of faith that seeks to glorify Him. This is what God commanded Adam to do in the garden of Eden. Close this lesson by reading Matthew 5:48 with your teacher.

Words you need to know from the Bible

Works   Acts that people do to complete a job

Perfectly   Without error; with no mistakes

37

Required   Something that must be done

Exactly   When something is correct in every detail

Lesson 3

Bible Story

Read the story of Uzzah as he failed to obey the Lord perfectly from 2 Samuel 6:1-7.

This Bible story helps us to understand that even one sin is enough to bring down God's anger. The people of Israel were warned not to touch the Ark of God. However, Uzzah felt it was wise to touch the Ark because he thought that the Ark might fall over if someone did not steady it. This man learned the hard way that it is better to obey God exactly as He requires, rather than do things simply because they seem right to us at the time.

Many people, even today, are not careful to obey God's commandments. They think that they know better than the Lord how things should be done. May God save us from trusting in our own wisdom and may He give us the desire to obey Him exactly as He has directed. Close this lesson by reading Proverbs 3:5-7 with your teacher.

Lesson 4

Written Exercise

Complete the sentences using the words below.

Uzzah	works	careful	perfectly

1. God made a covenant of _____ with Adam.

2. Many people today are not _____ to obey God.

3. The Lord required Adam to obey Him _____ .

4. _____ disobeyed God by touching the Ark of God.

Lesson 5

Activity

Color the picture of the Ark of God shown below.

Unit 17   Obedience Brings Life

Catechism Drill

25. **Question:** What did God promise in the covenant of works?

    Answer: To reward Adam with life if he obeyed Him.

26. **Question:** What did God threaten in the covenant of works?

    Answer: To punish Adam with death if he disobeyed.

Catechism Drill was memorized on _____ (date).

Scripture Reading

Read 1 Corinthians 15:21-22 and Genesis 3:22-24 with your teacher. These Bible verses teach us that man was given a clear choice between life and death. Adam understood that God would reward him with a wonderful life if he obeyed. Also, Adam knew that God would punish him with spiritual and physical death if he disobeyed. You may see this fact clearly by reading Genesis 2:15-17 with your teacher.

God did not force Adam to disobey. In fact, God made it easy for man to obey. The sad lesson that this unit teaches is that Adam chose to disobey simply because he wanted to rebel against the Lord. The same is true in our own lives. We freely chose to disobey because we like to disobey. Without Christ, all people are slaves to sin.

Words you need to know from the Bible

Reward	Something that we get in return for something we have done
Threaten	To warn someone that punishment is coming if they do not act a certain way
Punish	To cause a person to undergo pain, experience loss, or suffer for wrongdoing—even to the point of death
Rebel	To go against the rule of a person in authority

Lesson 3

Bible Story

Read the story of the two criminals who hung on the cross next to Jesus from Luke 23:20-43. This Bible story teaches us that people who do evil things deserve to get punished. Notice how the one criminal that hung next to Jesus on the cross refused to admit that he deserved to be punished. The other man, who was also a criminal, freely said that he was worthy to be killed because he did evil things. Jesus honored the man who confessed his sin and turned his heart toward God. Close this story by reading Romans 6:23 with your teacher.

Lesson 4

Written Exercise

Complete the sentences by using the words below.

chose	threatened	life	death

1. God promised to reward Adam with _____ if he obeyed.

2. Adam freely _____ to disobey the Lord.

3. The wages of sin is _____ .

4. God _____ to punish Adam with death if he disobeyed.

Lesson 5

Activity

Color the picture of the cross shown below.

Choose you this day whom you will serve.

But as for me and my house, we will serve the Lord.
—Joshua 24:15

Unit 18   Sin Breaks God's Law

Catechism Drill

27. **Question:** Did Adam keep the covenant of works?

    Answer: No, he sinned against God.

28. **Question:** What is sin?

    Answer: Any thought, word, or deed that breaks God's Law by omission or commission.

Catechism Drill was memorized on _____ (date).

Scripture Reading

Read Genesis 3:1-19 and 1 John 3:4. These Bible passages teach us that Adam sinned by not obeying God's command and did something that was forbidden. He ate the forbidden fruit. The Lord set down clear rules or laws for Adam to obey. Adam chose to break God's law and he became a sinner.

This first sin also broke the agreement or covenant that God had made with Adam. Because of this, Adam chose death rather than life. The things we choose to do, or not to do, are important! Whenever we choose to do something that God does not want us to do, we sin. Close this lesson by reading Proverbs 11:19 with your teacher.

Words you need to know from the Bible

Thought   Something our minds think about

Deed   An act or action taken by someone

Omission   To leave something out or undone

Commission   To do something on purpose after thinking about it

---

Lesson 3

Bible Story

Read Job Chapter One. This story helps us to see a person who was tempted to sin, but who was able to keep from evil. Job was tempted to sin by Satan. The devil took away most of the earthly things he had. Still, verses 21 and 22 tell us that Job did not sin in thought, word, or deed.

It would have been easy for Job to sin. However, the Holy Spirit gave him the strength and wisdom to resist sin and trust in God.

Lesson 4

Written Exercise

Complete the sentences using the words below.

Law	death	sinned	Job

1. Adam _____ and broke his covenant with God

2. _____ did not sin in thought, word, or deed after losing many things.

3. When we sin, we break God's _____ .

4. Adam chose the covenant of _____ .

Lesson 5

Activity

Help the children find their way to the Word of God.

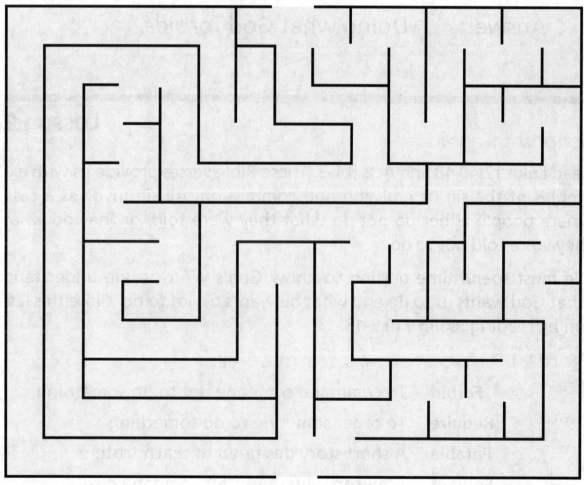

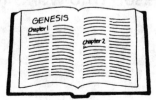

Unit 19   The Nature of Sin

Catechism Drill

29. Question: What is a sin of omission?

    Answer: Not being or doing
    what God requires.

30. Question: What is a sin of commission?

    Answer: Doing what God forbids.

Catechism Drill was memorized on _____ (date).

Scripture Reading

Read Luke 12:40-48 and Acts 8:1-3. These Bible verses provide us with examples of the sin of omission and commission. All sin involves a case where people either do not do what they were told, or they do what they were told not to do.

We must spend time getting to know God's Word so we understand what God wants us to do and what he wants us not to do. Close this lesson by reading Psalm 119:9-16.

Words you need to know from the Bible

Forbid   To command someone not to do something

Require   To order someone to do something

Parable   A short story designed to teach truth

Servant   A person who works for someone else

Lesson 3

Bible Story

Read the parable of the sheep and goats from Matthew 25:31-46. This Bible story helps us to understand the sin of omission. When we are too lazy or hardhearted to help people in need, we are sinning against the God of love. God's law commands us to love our neighbor as much as we love ourselves. When we refuse to love our neighbor, we break God's law and sin. Close this lesson by reading James 4:17 with your teacher.

Lesson 4

Written Exercise

Complete the sentences using the words below.

love	required	omission	good

1. The sin of _____ is not doing what God requires.

2. We are commanded to _____ our neighbor as ourselves.

3. To him that knoweth to do _____ and doeth it not, to him it is sin.

4. For unto whom much is given, much shall be _____ .

Lesson 5

Activity

Color the sheep yellow and help him find his way to his home in heaven. Can the goat find his way to heaven? (Read Matthew 25:31–33)

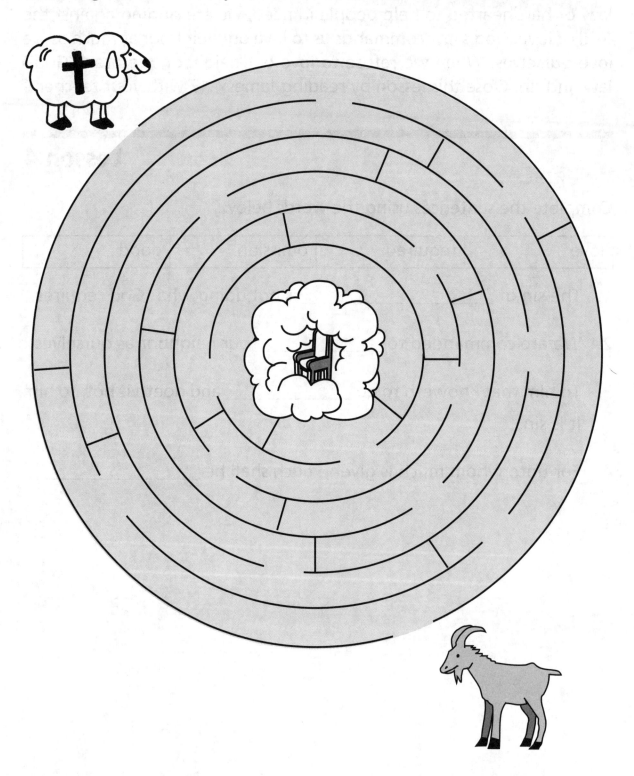

Unit 20   What Sin Deserves

Catechism Drill

31. Question: What does every sin deserve?

    Answer: The wrath and curse of God.

Catechism Drill was memorized on _____ (date)

Scripture Reading

Read John 3:36, Romans 6:23 and James 2:8-10. These Bible passages teach us that each and every sin committed by man deserves God's wrath. It was just one sin that caused all of mankind to fall under the curse of a Holy God. The Bible teaches us that if we sin in one area of God's law, we are guilty of breaking the whole law.

This truth is important to remember, for many people foolishly think that if they only sin a little bit, they do not need a Saviour. The truth is, every person stands guilty and under the wrath of a Holy God because all people are sinners. Everyone needs a Saviour, because no person can obey the Law of God perfectly and satisfy God's justice.

Words you need to know from the Bible

Deserve	To earn something
Wrath	Strong anger
Curse	To bring problems and trouble upon a person as a punishment
Foolishly	To act or think in an unwise manner
Saviour	A person who can free people from the curse and penalty of sin; Jesus is the only true Saviour.

49

Lesson 3

Bible Story

Read the Parable of the Prodigal Son from Luke 15:11-24. This wonderful story helps us to understand that every time we sin we offend God. Look at Luke 15:21 for a moment, and you will notice that the sinful son in the story says that he has "sinned against heaven." This simply means that he understood that all sins dishonor God.

Also this story teaches us that this sinner understood that he was not worthy to be blessed by his father. He knew that he deserved to be punished by a father who was justly angry. In the same way, all sinners must admit that they are not worthy of the mercy and love that God gives, even when they ask for forgiveness.

Lesson 4

Written Exercise

Complete the sentences using the words below.

God	Saviour	one	deserves

1. Every sin _____ the wrath and curse of God.

2. The Prodigal Son sinned against _____ and man.

3. It was just _____ sin that caused mankind to fall.

4. Everyone needs a _____ .

Activity

Complete the crossword puzzle. Try not to look back at the story of the Prodigal Son for your answers.

Word Bank

MONEY

WORTHY

EAT

TWO

SWINE

HUNGER

Clues

Across

1. The Prodigal Son said that he was not _____ to be called a son.

3. The foolish son who left home had to feed _____ .

5. After the son repented of his sin, the father said let us _____ and be merry.

Down

2. The Prodigal Son spent all of his _____ .

4. When the son came to his senses, he had a problem with _____ .

6. The father in the story had _____ sons.

Unit 21   Satan Is Our Enemy

Catechism Drill

32. Question: What was the original sin of our first parents?

      Answer: **Eating the forbidden fruit.**

33. Question: Who tempted them to this sin?

      Answer: **The devil tempted Eve, and she gave the fruit to Adam.**

Catechism Drill was memorized on _____ (date).

Scripture Reading

Read Genesis 3:1-6 and 1 Peter 5:8 with your teacher. These Bible verses teach us that Satan has been the enemy of mankind from the very beginning of the world. Today, Satan is especially the enemy of God's people and he seeks to bring everyone to hell with him.

The great sin of Eve was to doubt God when she listened to the words of the devil. The Bible warns us not to give Satan any place in our hearts. Once Eve disobeyed God by eating the fruit, she sinned. We can only guard our hearts with God's spiritual weapons against the temptations and evil tricks of Satan. Close this lesson by reading Ephesians 6:10–18 with your teacher.

Words you need to know from the Bible

Forbidden   When someone is told not to do something

Tempt   To try to make someone do wrong

Enemy   A person or group who does not like you

Careful   To be on guard against danger

Bible Story

Lesson 3

Read the Parable of the Tares from Matthew 13:24-30 and 36-43 with your teacher. This story helps us to see that the devil is the enemy of God and His people. Satan works to destroy the Kingdom of God by planting evil thoughts into the hearts of Christian people who are spiritually sleepy.

Do not be tricked into believing that you can be a friend of both the devil and God. If Jesus Christ is your friend, you must trust Him to protect you. Satan is your enemy and you should run away from his temptations.

Written Exercise

Lesson 4

Complete the sentences using the words below.

tempted	Satan	forbidden	careful

1. _____ is the enemy of all of God's people.

2. Adam ate the _____ fruit.

3. We must be _____ not to listen to the devil.

4. Satan _____ Eve first.

Activity

Lesson 5

Ask your teacher to help you plant a flower in a garden outside or in a flower pot. As you watch your flower grow, keep a careful eye out for weeds. If you see a weed growing near your flower, be sure to pull the weed out and get rid of it. This activity will help to remind you that weeds are like sin, and we must look to Jesus to pull out the sins that are rooted in our hearts.

Unit 22   Sin Brings Sadness

Catechism Drill

34. Question: What happened to Adam and Eve when they sinned?

    Answer: Instead of being holy and happy, they became sinful and miserable.

Catechism Drill was memorized on _____ (date).

Scripture Reading

Read Genesis 3:16-24 and Revelation 21:1-4. As we have already noted, Adam and Eve chose to sin. They lost their happiness and innocence when they sinned. God promised that Adam and Eve would die spiritually and physically if they disobeyed. The Lord always keeps His promises.

Many young people and adults do not like the fact that life is sometimes hard and full of sadness. Such people often become angry with God as if God was to blame. We must never forget that God is **not** to blame! People are sinful and sad by choice because all people chose to sin. Sickness, death, and pain are just some of the evil things that we face because of His curse on our sin.

The good news is that sinners can turn back to God through faith in Jesus Christ and receive a new life of peace and joy.

Words you need to know from the Bible

Miserable	Completely unhappy and very sad
Innocence	To be pure and free from sin
Blame	To put responsibility on someone for a sin or mistake
Promise	When someone says that he will do something

Lesson 3

Bible Story

Read the story of the birth of Christ from Luke 2:1-14. This story reminds us that the birth of Christ brought new hope and joy to a dark and sad world. Before Christ came as the Saviour of the world, the world was lost in sin and under the bondage of Satan.

The best gift that God ever gave to sinful people, is the gift of His only Son, Jesus Christ. If Jesus had never come into this world, all people would be lost in their sins and doomed to spend eternity in hell. Thanks be to God for sending Jesus to be the joy and light of the world. Close this lesson by reading 1 Peter 1:3-9 with your teacher.

Lesson 4

Written Exercise

Complete the sentences by using the words below.

miserable	blame	joy	promised

1. When Adam and Eve sinned, they became sinful

   and _____.

2. God _____ Adam and Eve that they would die if they

   disobeyed.

3. Sinful people sometimes try to _____ God for their

   sadness and trouble.

4. The angels sang a song of _____ when Jesus was born.

Lesson 5

Activity

Complete the crossword puzzle. Try not to look back at the story of Christ's birth from Luke Chapter two.

					4		
		2					
1							6
		3					
		5					

Word Bank

SHEPHERDS

BETHLEHEM

SAVIOUR

HOST

MARY

MANGER

Clues

Across

1. The angel of the Lord appeared to the _____ .

3. The angel was joined by the heavenly _____ to praise God.

5. The angel said that the Christ child would be lying in a _____ .

Down

2. Jesus was born in the city of _____ .

4. Jesus was the first born son of _____ .

6. Christ the Lord is the _____ of the world.

Unit 23　We Fell in Adam

Catechism Drill

35. Question:　Did Adam act for himself alone in the covenant of works?

    Answer:　No, he represented all of his descendants.

36. Question:　What did Adam's sin do to his descendents?

    Answer:　Everyone is born in a state of sin and guilt.

Catechism was memorized on _____ (date)

Scripture Reading

Read Romans 5:12-21 and 1 Corinthians 15:21-22 with your teacher. When our lesson says that Adam "represented" us in the garden of Eden, it means that he acted for us. In other words, Adam, like a king or president, did not act for himself alone. His sin had serious results for himself and for everybody else who would be born after him; his descendants.

All people are descendants of Adam and Eve and share in the guilt of his sin. Everyone (except Jesus) has been born in a state of sin because God has judged all who are children of Adam with the sentence of death. We do not need to work at becoming a sinner. We all by nature find it easy to sin because we are born dead in our sins and spiritually blind. We are unable to do anything good apart from God's grace. We are slaves of sin.

Words you need to know from the Bible

Descendants	People who are born from a particular person
Guilty	When someone is found to have broken a moral or civil law
Represented	When a person acts on behalf of others or takes the place of others
Sin	Breaking God's law or failing to obey what it tells us to do
Generate	Give birth to another person

Lesson 3

Bible Story

Read the story of how Adam and Eve generated the families of the earth in Genesis Chapters 4 and 5. This Bible passage helps us to understand how God used Adam and Eve to greatly increase the human race.

As you can see from this passage, Eve had many children. Our first parents, Adam and Eve, had many children to follow them as their descendants. However, we should also note that each child that was born had a sinful heart. The boy named Cain is a good example of how wickedness had entered into the hearts of men. This was just what God promised would happen! Also, just as God promised, Adam would himself die. We read about the death of Adam in Genesis 5:5.

Lesson 4

Written Exercise

Complete the sentences using the words below.

guilty	Cain	represented	Adam

1. Adam _____ all of his descendants in the garden.
2. The sin of Adam made all people _____ and sinful.
3. After 930 years, _____ finally died.
4. Wicked _____ killed his brother Abel.

Lesson 5

Activity

With your teacher's help, fill in the chart below to help you see the line of descendants in your family.

Your Family Tree

ADAM AND EVE
OUR FIRST PARENTS

GREAT-GREAT GRANDPARENTS

GREAT-GREAT GRANDPARENTS

GREAT GRANDPARENTS

GREAT GRANDPARENTS

GRANDPARENTS

GRANDPARENTS

FATHER

MOTHER

YOUR NAME

Unit 24 How Bad Is Sin?

Catechism Drill

37. Question: How sinful are you by nature?

    Answer: I inherit original sin and am corrupt in every part of my being.

Catechism Drill was memorized on _____ (date).

Scripture Reading

Read Psalm 51:1-5 and 1 John 1:5-10 with your teacher. These Scripture passages teach us that everyone is born with a completely corrupt nature. The fall of the human race was so complete, that people are unable to keep from living a sinful life. Every part of man was affected by the fall of our covenant head, Adam, in the original sin. People are unable to do anything good in their own strength because of the fall.

However, God in His mercy has not permitted all people to be as bad as they can be. They have not yet become like Satan himself. For the devil does not even act good some of the time. He is as evil as can be all the time. Although every part of man has been corrupted by sin, God keeps people from sinning as much as they want. If God let people act as bad as they are all the time, the world would be so violent that the gospel could not be preached.

Words you need to know from the Bible

Nature	The way you are made
Corrupt	Affected by the evil of sin
Being	The whole of a person in body and spirit
Restrain	To keep someone from doing anything they wish

Original Sin   Adam's first sin which brought guilt and corruption to all of his descendents

Bible Story

Read the story of Korah's wicked rebellion against Moses from Numbers 16. This Bible story gives us a true example of how God takes an active role in His world to restrain wicked people from doing what they want. Foolish sinners often desire things that are bad for them and God.

Whenever we ask God for anything, we must always be quick to say that we only want it if God thinks it is good. We should always pray that the Lord's will would be done, because God alone knows what is best. As fallen sinners, we can never trust our mind and heart. God alone can be trusted to do what is right.

Written Exercise

Complete the sentences using the words below.

Satan	Korah	trust	corrupt

1. All people are _____ by nature.

2. Only _____ is as sinful as he can be.

3. God stopped _____ from doing evil against Moses.

4. Fallen sinners can never _____ their own minds or hearts.

Lesson 5

Activity

With your teacher's help, complete the following activity so you can better understand the extent of man's corruption in sin.

Start by getting three small clear glasses. Put pure and clean water in the first glass. Put clean water in the second glass, but add a few drops of dark food coloring and some dirt in the bottom, but do <u>not</u> stir it up. In the third glass, do the same but stir it up and add lots of dark coloring.

The first glass is like Adam before he sinned, pure and holy. The second glass is like fallen man today, because the ugly coloring of sin has completely filled the glass and it is not fit for drinking. However, the third glass is like Satan and those who are in hell today. This last glass is as bad and dirty as it can be. Ask your teacher to help you if you still have questions about this lesson.

PURE AND SINLESS

CORRUPTED BY SIN IN EVERY PART

EVIL AS CAN BE

Unit 25   You Must Be Born Again

Catechism Drill

38. Question: Can you go to heaven with this sinful nature?

    Answer: No, my heart must be changed before I can be fit for heaven.

39. Question: What is this change of heart called?

    Answer: The new birth, or regeneration.

40. Question: Who is able to change your heart?

    Answer: The Holy Spirit alone.

Catechism Drill was memorized on _____ (date).

Scripture Reading

Read Titus 3:1-7 and John 1:6-13 with your teacher. Sinful men are not interested in loving and serving God. People lost in their sins do not have a heart for God and do not wish to make themselves holy on God's terms. Most sinners want to go to heaven, but they do not want to change or repent from their sinful ways and trust in Jesus Christ.

The sad fact is that people who try to get to heaven with a sinful heart will not get in. God must give us a new heart of faith before we can enter heaven. It is God the Holy Spirit who breathes new spiritual life into each person saved by Christ. He brings the light of the gospel to them and draws them to Christ. No human work, not even tears and crying, can make a person fit for heaven. A Holy God must pour out mercy and grace through His Spirit upon each soul that is saved, for man cannot save himself.

63

Words you need to know from the Bible

Fit	To be prepared
Regeneration	Spiritual rebirth by the Holy Spirit
Terms	The guidelines or rules of an agreement
Repent	To turn away from error unto the truth

Lesson 3

Bible Story

Read the story of Jesus and Nicodemus from John 3:1-21 with your teacher. Before anyone can be ready to receive the gift of eternal life, they must be "born again" (or "born from above"). Jesus taught Nicodemus that this "new birth" involves an act of God giving to a person a new spiritual life. The Lord does not make us babies again by giving us tiny bodies when we are born again. He gives us ears to hear His Word and a new heart to believe the Gospel so that we might become alive in Christ.

We receive the gift of God's love through the Holy Spirit. He gives us the gift of faith in order that we might believe in Jesus as Lord and Saviour.

Lesson 4

Written Exercise

Complete the sentences using the words below.

Nicodemus	regeneration	heaven	Holy Spirit

1. Only the _____ _____ can change your heart.

2. No person can go to _____ with a sinful nature.

3. Jesus taught _____ about salvation by the new birth.

4. The new birth or change of heart is called _____ .

Lesson 5

Activity

With your teacher's help, purchase or borrow a battery operated flashlight. After you get the flashlight, leave it on until the batteries are dead. Ask your teacher to "replace" the batteries so the flashlight has new life and can be useful again. After the new batteries are in, turn the flashlight on again so you can see the new light it has.

This activity will help you to see a simple example of what spiritual regeneration is like. When Adam sinned, he lost all power to obey God rightly. He no longer had the light of God burning in his soul. He became useless to serve a Holy God. It is only after God powerfully changes or regenerates a person's heart that good works will shine forth. Jesus Christ is the power of God and the light of the world. No one can enjoy a new life unless Christ first raises him from spiritual death by the power of the Holy Spirit.

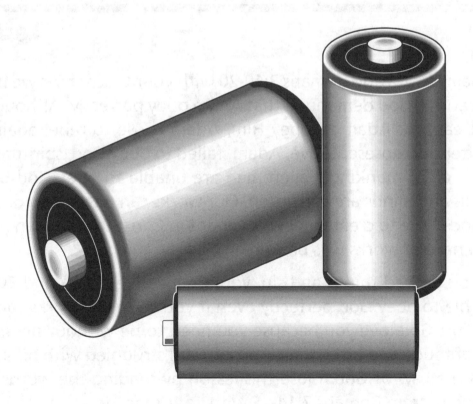

Unit 26   Works Will Not Save

Catechism Drill

41. Question: Can you be saved through
                 the covenant of works?

    Answer: No, because I broke it
                 and am condemned by it.

42. Question: How did you break
                 the covenant of works?

    Answer: Adam represented me,
                 and so I fell with him in his first sin.

Catechism was memorized on _____ (date).

Scripture Reading

Read Psalm 14:1-3 and Romans 3:10-20 with your teacher. As we have already learned, God demanded that Adam obey perfectly. Although God made it easy for Adam to obey Him, Adam chose to rebel against the Lord. After our representative, Adam, failed to obey God, spiritual death fell upon all of mankind. Fallen men are unable to obey God because their wills and minds are corrupted. Our works can never save our guilty souls. God chose to create a new covenant in Christ to save men because the covenant of works was broken.

When you do bad things and sin, you are just like Adam and Eve. You are unable to obey God perfectly even if you try. Your works can never make a just God love you because you need to be without sin and perfectly righteous. Even the great Apostle Paul struggled with his inability to keep the Law of God. Close this lesson by reading the words of the Apostle Paul from Romans 7:14-25 with your teacher.

Words you need to know from the Bible

Condemned	To be sentenced for breaking the law
Works	The things we do and say
Perfectly	When something is done without error or mistakes
Will	The part of a person that chooses how to act and think

Lesson 3

Bible Story

Read the story of Christ walking on the water from Matthew 14:22-33. This story teaches us that people cannot save themselves by their own actions. Sin makes people doubt and dishonor God by showing a lack of faith in Him. Peter meant well as he asked to come to Jesus. But he turned his eyes away from Jesus and began to sink in the water. He failed to put complete trust in Jesus for a moment. As he sank he then cried out for the Lord to save him. In the same way we need to trust in Christ completely all the time and not trust in or fear anything else.

Lesson 4

Written Exercise

Complete the sentences using the words below.

fell	save	slave	condemned

1. All people have been _____ under the covenant of works.

2. All human beings _____ with Adam in his first sin.

3. The Bible teaches that fallen man is a _____ to sin.

4. Christ had to reach out and _____ Peter because he turned his eyes from Christ and began to fear the waves.

Activity

Complete the crossword puzzle. Try not to look back at the story of Christ walking on the water from Matthew Chapter 14.

Word Bank

CHEER

TOSSED

DISCIPLES

PETER

HAND

SINK

Clues

Across

1. Jesus directed the _____ to get in a ship.

3. The ship began to be _____ by the waves.

5. Jesus stretched forth His _____ to save Peter.

Down

2. Jesus told his disciples to be of good _____ .

4. _____ asked if he could come to Jesus on the water.

6. Peter became afraid and began to _____ into the water.

Unit 27 Catechism Review

Lesson 1
General Review

Review catechism questions 22-42 with your teacher. Do your best to memorize each of these questions along with the proper answers. If you are able to answer all of the questions, you may ask your teacher to give you an Outstanding Achievement Award.

Catechism Review was successfully completed on _____(date).

Lesson 2
Review Exercise (Catechism Questions 22-26)

Complete the sentences using the words below.

death	works	promises	chose	rainbow

1. The Lord always does what He _____ .

2. The _____ is a sign of God's covenant with Noah.

3. God made a covenant of _____ with Adam.

4. The wages of sin is _____ .

5. Adam freely _____ to disobey the Lord.

Lesson 3
Review Exercise (Catechism Questions 27-31)

Complete the sentences using the words below.

omission	one	God	required	Law

1. When we sin, we break God's _____ .

2. The sin of _____ is not doing what God requires.

69

3. For unto whom much is given, much shall be _____ .

4. The Prodigal Son sinned against _____ and man.

5. It was just _____ sin that caused mankind to fall.

Lesson 4

Review Exercise (Catechism Questions 32-36)

Complete the sentences using the words below.

careful	blame	joy	represented	Satan

1. _____ is the enemy of all of God's children.

2. We must be _____ not to listen to the devil.

3. Sinful people sometimes try to _____ God for their sadness and trouble.

4. The angels sang a song of _____ when Jesus was born.

5. Adam _____ all of his descendants.

Lesson 5

Review Exercise (Catechism Questions 37-41)

Complete the sentences using the words below.

trust	heaven	regeneration	Satan	fell

1. Only _____ is as sinful as can be.

2. Fallen sinners can never _____ their own heart.

3. No person can go to _____ with a sinful nature.

4. The new birth or change of heart is called _____ .

5. All human beings _____ with Adam in his first sin.

Unit 28   How To Be Saved

Catechism Drill

43. Question: How, then, can you be saved?

    Answer: By faith in the Lord Jesus Christ who fulfilled the covenant of grace.

Catechism Drill was memorized on _____ (date).

Scripture Reading

Read Ephesians 2:1-9 and Romans 5:17-21 with your teacher. Since fallen man was unable to do anything to save himself, God chose to make a way for people to be saved from the curse of sin. God decided to save out of the world a special people for His own possession. He chose to save them from their sins by way of a new covenant of grace. In this new covenant, God the Father sent his only Son into the world to pay the penalty for sin. This required the Son of God to be born as a man, to live a sinless life, and to die for the sins of His people.

As we learned before, the covenant of works was broken by Adam and the penalty was physical and spiritual death. Man, therefore, needed a Saviour who was both a sinless man and almighty God. For God would not accept the works of any man who was himself a sinner, and a mere man is not able to satisfy the wrath of God. Jesus is just the right kind of Saviour for He is both perfect man and perfect God.

Under this new covenant, God gives the gift of faith through the Holy Spirit to His chosen people so that they can believe in the work of Christ as Saviour. God now commands all men everywhere to repent and trust in the Son of God, Jesus Christ, in order to be saved. Salvation under the new covenant is by grace alone, through faith alone and in the crucified and risen Saviour Jesus Christ alone.

Salvation, therefore, is totally a work and gift of God and not of men. Our duty is to believe in Jesus as the only Saviour and to follow Him as Lord. God so loved the world that He gave his only begotten Son, that whosoever believes in Him shall not perish but have eternal life. (John 3:16)

Words you need to know from the Bible

Saved   To be freed from the power and penalty of sin

Grace   The free, undeserved mercy and redemptive love of God given through the Holy Spirit

Penalty   A punishment given to someone for breaking a law or agreement

Saviour   A person who is able to deliver people from sin and its penalty

Lesson 3

Bible Story

Read the story of Lydia and the story of the Philippian Jailer from Acts 16:9-34 with your teacher. This Bible story gives a clear example of the way of salvation. The Apostle Paul and Silas told the Philippian jailer and his family that the way to be saved was by believing in the Lord Jesus Christ. God opened the heart of Lydia, just like He did with the jailer and his family, to believe the Word of Christ as it was being preached.

Lesson 4

Written Exercise

Complete the sentences using the words below.

sinless	grace	penalty	believe

1. The new covenant is the covenant of _____ .

2. People are saved as they _____ on the Lord Jesus Christ.

3. The Saviour of men needed to be a _____ man himself.

4. Jesus Christ, our Saviour, saves us from the _____ and power of sin.

Activity

Lesson 5

Connect the dots shown below to reveal the picture. (Connect the dots from 1 through 9 and then start over with 1 again.)

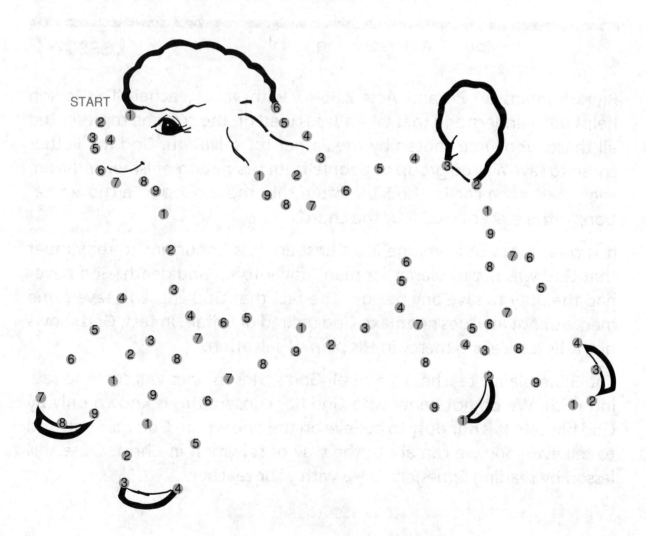

Jesus is the lamb of God

Unit 29   God's Chosen People

Catechism Drill

44. Question: Who did Jesus Christ represent
in the covenant of grace?

    Answer: **His elect people.**

Catechism Drill was memorized on _____ (date).

Scripture Reading

Read Romans 9:1-24 and Acts 2:36-47 with your teacher. This lesson helps us to understand that when Jesus died on the cross he represented all those who were chosen by the Father for salvation. God the Father chose to save a large group of people from the nation of Israel and from every nation on earth. The Bible often calls these people "a chosen nation," "the elect of God," or the church.

It is clear that not everyone is a Christian. It is important to remember that God was not to blame for man's fall into sin and death. God never had the duty to save any person. The fact that God chose to save some men, but not all, does not make God unkind or unfair. In fact, God shows both His justice and mercy in His plan of salvation.

The Bible plainly teaches us that all God's chosen ones will come to saving faith. We do not know who God has chosen, this is known only by God himself. It is our duty to believe on the one whom God has sent, and to tell everyone we can about the way of salvation in Christ. Close this lesson by reading Ephesians 1:1-6 with your teacher.

Words you need to know from the Bible

Elect   God's chosen people

Chosen   To pick out

Adopted   When someone is taken into a family by choice

74

Pleasure   Something that makes you happy

Lesson 3

Bible Story

Read the story about Jesus praying before his disciples from John 17:1-11 with your teacher. Jesus prays in this Bible story for the people whom His father has given Him to save. The Saviour Jesus Christ does not pray for every person in the world; He prays only for those whom His father gave Him to save, His church. Jesus knew exactly who He was dying for on the cross. Like the High Priest in the Old Testament, Jesus bore the names of His brethren before God (Exodus 28:29–30).

Lesson 4

Written Exercise

Complete the sentences using the words below.

grace	adopted	save	chosen

1. God has always had a _____ people.
2. Jesus represented the elect in the covenant of _____ .
3. All people chosen for salvation are _____ like children.
4. God never had the duty to _____ any person.

Lesson 5

Activity

The Bible teaches us that all men have sinned and fall short of the glory of God. No person deserves to be loved by God because all people are sinners. When God chooses to set His love upon any person, it is not because they are better, smarter or nicer than some other person. It is not because God looks ahead and sees that we believe out of ourselves. When someone is saved by God's grace, he should realize that God alone has saved them by His own hand.

To help you understand this truth, ask your teacher to help you find three or four toys or cups that look exactly the same. Set the items that look alike in front of you and have your teacher chose one or two of those items. This simple activity shows us that your teacher chose certain of the items only because it pleased him or her. The items themselves looked and acted exactly the same. The reason then for the choice was simply because that was the way the teacher wanted it.

God does the choosing of his spiritual children on the basis of His perfect will. It is the duty of Christians to tell everyone about their need to trust in Christ as Saviour and let God give the gift of faith to whomever He wishes.

Unit 30   God's Work of Grace

Catechism Drill

45. Question: What work did Jesus do in the
    covenant of grace?

    Answer: He kept the whole law for his people,
    and then was punished
    for all of their sins.

46. Question: Did Jesus ever sin?

    Answer: No, he lived a holy and sinless life.

Catechism Drill was memorized on _____ (date).

Lesson 2

Scripture Reading

Read Hebrews 4:14-16 and 1 Peter 2:17-24 with your teacher. The Bible teaches us that Christ came to do what Adam failed to do. The Lord Jesus Christ came to satisfy the righteous demands of God's law by leading a sinless life. He also came to destroy the works of the devil and to set His spiritual brethren free by satisfying God's wrath against sin.

When Jesus, the sinless Saviour, died on the cross, He paid the penalty for man's sin. God, in His mercy, sent His Son into the world to save lost and helpless sinners like you and me.

Words you need to know from the Bible

Whole	Something or someone is complete in every part
Work	When action is taken to do something
Kept	To put something under your control and protect it perfectly
Sinless	Free from sin in mind and heart

Lesson 3

Bible Story

Read the story about Christ before Pontius Pilate from Luke 23:1-47 with your teacher. This Bible story tells us that Jesus went to the cross as an innocent man. No honest person, not even Pilate, could find sin or fault with Jesus. The Lord Jesus Christ, a just and perfect man, suffered a cruel death so that those who believe in him would not have to die in their sins and go to hell.

Lesson 4

Written Exercise

Complete the sentences using the words below.

fault	punished	whole	sinless

1. Jesus kept the _____ law for His people.

2. Pontius Pilate could not find _____ with Jesus.

3. Jesus was _____ for all of the sins of His people.

4. The Lord Jesus lived a _____ life.

Lesson 5

Activity

Complete the crossword puzzle. Try not to look back at the story of Christ before Pilate from Luke Chapter 23.

Word Bank

BARABBAS

KING

HEROD

CALVARY

CRUCIFY

PILATE

Clues

Across

1. The sign placed on the cross said that Jesus was _____ of the Jews.

3. The crowd called for Pilate to release _____ .

5. The angry crowd cried out, " _____ Him! Crucify Him!"

Down

2. _____ said that he could find no fault in Jesus.

4. Jesus was sent to a place called _____ to be crucified.

6. King _____ also found nothing in Jesus that made Him worthy of death.

Unit 31   Christ Was Born to Suffer

Catechism Drill

47. Question: How could the Son of God suffer?

   Answer: The Son of God became a true man so that He could obey and suffer.

48. Question: For whom did Christ obey and suffer?

   Answer: For all who were given to Him by the Father.

49. Question: What kind of life did Christ live on earth?

   Answer: A life of poverty and suffering.

Catechism Drill was memorized on _____ (date).

Scripture Reading

Read Isaiah 53:1-10 and 1 Peter 3:17-18 with your teacher. The Son of God, Jesus Christ, is the creator of the world and is all-powerful. No man or group of men can hurt Him or make Him sad because He controls all things from heaven above. The Lord Jesus also owns everything in heaven and earth so He is very rich as well.

The Son of God, in obedience to His Father, chose to leave His glorious and peaceful home in heaven to become a man. No person forced Jesus to leave His riches and beautiful home. He left heaven to live as a poor and humble man, to suffer pain and death. He did this simply because He was obedient to His Father in offering Himself in the place of those given to Him by God.

The Lord Jesus went through a great deal of pain and trouble to save lost sinners. Close this lesson by reading John 6:41-47 with your teacher.

Words you need to know from the Bible

Suffer   To go through pain

Earth   The name given to the world we live on

Poverty   When someone is poor and lives with very little

Peaceful   Quiet and calm

Lesson 3

Bible Story

Read the story of Jesus and the excited followers from Matthew 8:18-23 with your teacher. This short Bible story teaches an important truth.

We need to have more than a little interest in serving God, for anyone who follows God faithfully will suffer. The men in this story wanted to follow Jesus until they found out that Jesus lived a hard life of poverty. After they understood that they would have to give up their worldly riches or pleasures to follow Christ, they lost interest in following the Lord. We must count the cost and follow God with all of our heart.

Lesson 4

Written Exercise

Complete the sentences using the words below.

poverty	man	forced	pain

1. The Son of God had to suffer as a sinless _____ .
2. Jesus lived a life of _____ and suffering.
3. The Son of God had to go through a great deal of _____ to save lost sinners.
4. No person _____ Jesus to leave His beautiful home in heaven.

Lesson 5

Activity

To remind you of the teaching of Christ regarding His poverty on earth, ask your teacher to help you find a bird's nest. Study the interesting way in which birds make their humble little homes.

If you are unable to find a bird's nest, you can make a bird house. Simply ask your teacher to help you build a birdhouse with wood and nails.

After you are finished with this activity, read Matthew 8:20 with your teacher. You may also wish to print this Bible verse on the side of your birdhouse if you decide to make this project.

Unit 32   Jesus Paid for Sin

Catechism Drill

50. **Question:**   What kind of death did Jesus die?

    Answer: The painful and shameful
                     death of the cross.

51. **Question:**   What is meant by the atonement?

    Answer: Christ paid the full penalty for
                     sinners by His suffering and death,
                     thus satisfying God's justice.

Catechism Drill was memorized on _____ (date).

Lesson 2

Scripture Reading

Read Matthew 27:22-50 and 1 Corinthians 15:1-6 with your teacher. Christ suffered on the cross to pay for sin so that whosoever believes in Him could be accepted by God. Because God is just He demanded a perfect sacrifice for sin. That is why Jesus went to the cross. Only Jesus could provide a perfect sacrifice to God because He was without sin.

As we read the story of Christ going to the cross, we see how much pain and sadness he had to go through. Jesus went through all this because He knew that God could never be friends with sinners until He had paid God's penalty for sin in full. Jesus paid the penalty which is death. If we trust in Him, we will be forgiven and the curse of death will be removed. Close this lesson by reading John 15:12-17 with your teacher.

Words you need to know from the Bible

Painful   When we are hurt and feeling bad

Shameful   That which makes one look foolish or immoral

Atonement   When someone pays a penalty that should have been paid by others

Accepted   To receive something offered

Bible Story

Read the story of Abraham offering Isaac from Genesis 22:1-18 with your teacher. This story helps us to understand how God provided atonement for the sins of His people. God asked Abraham to offer up his son Isaac to die as an offering for sin. Abraham trusted God to provide some animal to take the place of his son, Isaac. The wrath and anger of a holy God would be put upon an animal instead of upon Isaac, because Abraham believed in the faithfulness of God. The Lord blessed Abraham for his faith and obedience by saving his only son, Isaac.

If we trust in Jesus, He takes our place on the cross. Then we do not have to give our lives as an offering for sin and die. The holy anger of God was poured out upon Christ instead of upon guilty sinners like you and me.

Written Exercise

Complete the sentences using the words below.

penalty	shameful	atonement	offer

1. People who die on a cross suffer a _____ death.

2. Jesus paid the full _____ for our sin.

3. The _____ of Christ made it possible for God's people to live forever with Him.

4. Abraham was willing to _____ up Isaac because he trusted God to be good.

Lesson 5

Activity

Color the picture below of Abraham and Isaac in the wilderness.

Unit 33   God Saves Sinners

Catechism Drill

52. Question: What did God the Father promise to do in the covenant of grace?

    Answer: To justify, sanctify and glorify all those for whom Christ died.

53. Question: What is justification?

    Answer: It is God's forgiving sinners and treating them as if they had never sinned.

54. Question: What is sanctification?

    Answer: It is God's making sinners holy in heart and conduct.

Catechism Drill was memorized on _____(date).

Scripture Reading

Read Ephesians 1:3–5, 2:1-10 and Romans 8:28-33 with your teacher. God the Father chose to save believers from the punishment they deserve and make them holy. Because of the work of Jesus, God treats those who believe in Christ as if they have never sinned. This is because each person who becomes a Christian receives the gift of the righteousness of Christ. His righteousness covers them like a blanket covers a little baby. God loves those who are covered by the righteous works of Jesus. He forgives them and treats them as righteous because their sins are covered by the blood of Jesus.

He also makes them holy in the way they think and act, because they have the Holy Spirit living in them. When God saves people, He also begins to make them think and act like His Son, Jesus Christ. All of God's people are created in Christ Jesus unto good works.

Words you need to know from the Bible

Justify	To defend or uphold as right
Sanctify	To make someone or something holy and pure
Holy	Pure and dedicated to God
Deserve	When a person gets what he should rightly receive

Lesson 3

Bible Story

Read the story of how God saved Saul from Acts 9:1-22 with your teacher. This Bible story shows us the power of God in salvation. God not only saved the wicked sinner named Saul, but He turned him into a holy and bold servant of Christ. The Lord forgave Saul and gave him a new heart that loved to share the good news of Christ with other people.

Lesson 4

Written Exercise

Complete the sentences using the words below.

Sanctification	justify	holy	never

1. God the Father promised to _____ and sanctify all of His elect.

2. The Lord treats His children as if they had _____ sinned.

3. _____ happens as God makes sinners holy in heart and conduct.

4. God saved Saul and made him a _____ man.

Lesson 5

Activity

Complete the crossword puzzle. Try not to look at Acts Chapter 9.

Word Bank

PREACHED

BAPTIZED

DAMASCUS

TARSUS

JESUS

ANANIAS

CLUES

Across

1. Saul came from the city of _____ .

3. As Saul came near _____ , a bright light shined upon him.

5. After Saul received his sight, he was _____ .

Down

2. It was _____ who spoke with Saul on the road to Damascus.

4. God sent a disciple named _____ to visit Saul in Damascus.

6. Soon after Saul was saved, he _____ Christ in the synagogues.

Unit 34   Turn from Sin to Christ

Catechism Drill

55. Question: Who will be saved?

    Answer: Only those who repent of sin, believe in Christ, and lead holy lives.

56. Question: How do you repent of your sins?

    Answer: By being sorry enough for my sin to hate and forsake it.

57. Question: Why must you hate and forsake your sin?

    Answer: Because it displeases God.

Catechism Drill was memorized on _____ (date).

Scripture Reading

Read Isaiah 55:6-7 and Psalm 97:10 with your teacher. The Bible makes it clear that no man can serve two masters. We cannot serve both God and the devil. Therefore, when we come to God by faith in Christ, we must put off our old way of life when we served sin and Satan. We must repent from our sinful ways and seek to please God in all that we do.

To repent means to be sorry for our sin and to turn from it because it displeases God. To believe in Christ is to believe what the Bible says about our sin as well as what Christ did on the cross.

Words you need to know from the Bible

Repent To be sorry for sin and to turn away from it

Forsake To leave something behind

89

Displeases   Something that makes a person sad or angry

Hate   To dislike someone or something very much

Lesson 3

Bible Story

Read the story of Lot's wife from Genesis 19:1-26 with your teacher. This Bible story teaches us that when we leave our old life of sin we must not look back and want to be that way again.

Lot lived in a wicked city called Sodom. This city was a city of sin. Lot was told by two angels to take his wife and children out of Sodom. The angels helped Lot and his family to get out of the city and God warned them not to look back. However, Lot's wife disobeyed and looked back at the city of Sodom. God turned her into a pillar of salt.

Many people living today are just like Lot's wife. They do not completely turn away from their old life of sin. Rather, they still go back to their old sinful ways. God tells us that if we have a new life in Christ, we will not go back to our old way of living. We will hate sin and refuse to go back.

Lesson 4

Written Exercise

Complete the sentences using the words below.

displeases	Sodom	repent	forsake

1. We must _____ of sin and believe in Christ to be saved.

2. All sin _____ God.

3. We must hate sin and _____ it.

4. Lot's wife disobeyed God by looking back at sinful _____ .

Activity

To help you remember the Bible story about Lot's wife, try the following project.

Start by locating one long pipe cleaner about 12 inches long, or two twisted together. You will also need five short pipe cleaners about four inches long. Bend the longest cleaner into a "U" shape. Pinch and twist the top inch of the cleaner so it forms a head and once around the middle to make the hips. Twist one small pipe cleaner around the neck area for arms. Wrap the remaining pipe cleaners around the body in a circular motion to fill the figure out. Paint the figure with glue and roll it in salt. Mount this image by drilling two small holes in a block of wood for the legs to fit in.

Put this salty figure in your bedroom to remind you that you must never turn back to your old life of sin when you became a child of God.

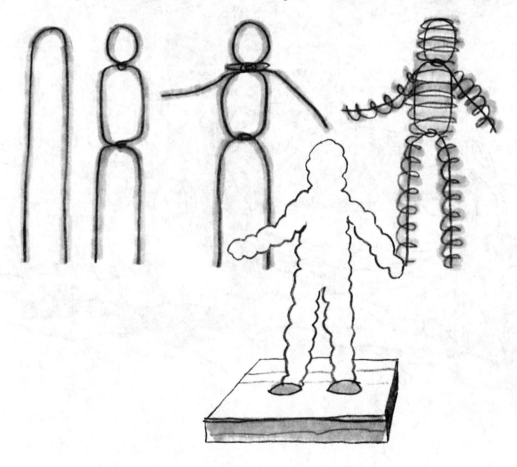

Extra Activity

This unit presented the truth that God is pleased when His children obey Him. Christians must hate sin and follow God's Holy Word. The Lord Jesus Christ once said "...Man shall not live by bread alone, but by every word that proceedeth out of the mouth of God." (Matthew 4:4)

If you would like to do an extra project, ask one of your teachers to help you bake a loaf of bread. After the bread has been baked, ask your teacher to help you put the following words on top of your bread; "Man shall not live by bread alone." You should use regular icing to put down the words on your loaf of bread. At the close of your project, ask your teacher to let you have a piece of bread after you read Matthew 4:4.

Unit 35   Trust in Christ Alone

Catechism Drill

58. Question: What is it to believe or have faith in Christ?

      Answer: To trust in Christ alone for salvation.

59. Question: Can you repent and believe in Christ by your own power?

      Answer: No, I can do nothing good without the help of God's Holy Spirit.

60. Question: How can you receive the help of the Holy Spirit?

      Answer: God has told us that we must pray to Him for the Holy Spirit.

Catechism Drill was memorized on _____ (date).

Scripture Reading

Read John 14:1-21, Acts 16:14-15, and Luke 11:9-13 with your teacher. The Bible teaches us that there is only one way to come to God and be saved. Jesus himself in John chapter 14 says that He is "<u>the</u> way, <u>the</u> truth, and <u>the</u> life…". Jesus did not simply say that He was one of the ways to God. He said that He was <u>the only way</u> to God. Christ alone can save our souls.

The third person of the Trinity, the Holy Spirit, opens hearts to believe in the Lord Jesus Christ. The woman Lydia, in the book of Acts, believed when God opened her heart by the Holy Spirit. When we believe in Christ we should know that it is because God opened our hard heart and created faith within. Salvation comes through the power of God, for all power in heaven and on earth belongs to God. Only the Holy Spirit, not our efforts, can break through our stony hearts of sin.

Words you need to know from the Bible

Believe   To accept something as true

Pray   When someone talks with God

Salvation   The act whereby God gives new spiritual life to someone

Lydia   A Christian woman who lived during the time of the Apostle Paul.

Lesson 3

Bible Story

Read the story of Christ the Good Shepherd from John 10:1-16. Sheep are weak and fearful animals that often loose their way. The Lord Jesus used this animal to describe sinful man. All people are spiritually dead and unable to find their way to God. Only Christ, the Good Shepherd can find lost sinners and lead them into the green pastures of God's love and grace.

Lesson 4

Written Exercise

Complete the sentences using the words below.

life	sheep	trust	good

1. We must _____ in Christ alone for salvation.

2. Jesus is the way, the truth, and the _____ .

3. The Bible says that we are like _____ .

4. We can do nothing _____ without the help of the Holy Spirit.

Lesson 5

Activity

Color the picture of the sheep below and paste cotton balls onto this picture.

"All we like sheep have gone astray; everyone of us has turned to his own way; but the Lord has laid on Him the iniquity of us all." —Isaiah 53:6

Unit 36   Catechism Review

Lesson 1

Review Catechism questions 43-60 with your teacher. Do your best to memorize each of these questions along with the proper answers. If you are able to answer all of the questions, you may ask your teacher to give you an Outstanding Achievement Award.

Catechism Review was successfully completed on _____(date).

Lesson 2

Review Exercise (Catechism Questions 42-46)

Complete the sentences using the words below.

chosen	whole	grace	save	fell

1. All human beings _____ with Adam in his first sin.

2. The new covenant is the covenant of _____ .

3. God has always had a _____ people.

4. Jesus kept the _____ law for His people.

5. God never had the duty to _____ any person.

Lesson 3

Review Exercise (Catechism Questions 47-51)

Complete the sentences using the words below.

shameful	atonement	forced	offer	poverty

1. Jesus lived a life of _____ and suffering.

2. No person _____ Jesus to leave His beautiful home in heaven.

3. People who die on the cross suffer a _____ death.

4. The _____ of Christ made it possible for God's people to live forever with God.

5. Abraham was willing to _____ up Isaac because he trusted God to be good.

Lesson 4

Review Exercise (Catechism Questions 52-56)

Complete the sentences using the words below.

never	justify	repent	Sodom	displeases

1. God the Father promised to _____ and sanctify all of His elect.

2. We must _____ of sin and believe in Christ to be saved.

3. The Lord treats His children as if they had _____ sinned.

4. All sin _____ God.

5. Lot's wife disobeyed God by looking back at sinful _____ .

Lesson 5

Review Exercise (Catechism Questions 57-60)

Complete the sentences using the words below.

life	good	sheep	forsake

1. We must hate sin and _____ it.

2. The Bible says that we are like _____ .

3. Jesus is the way, the truth, and the _____ .

4. We can do nothing _____ without the help of the Holy Spirit.

Outstanding Achievement

Award

Presented to:

for
Exceptional Work in

Memorizing Catechism Questions 1-21

During the Week of

Train up a child in the
way he should go, and
when he is old, he will
not depart from it.
Proverbs 22:6

———————————————

———————————————
Teacher's Signature

Outstanding Achievement

Award

Presented to:

for
Exceptional Work in

Memorizing Catechism Questions 22-42

During the Week of

Train up a child in the
way he should go, and
when he is old, he will
not depart from it.
Proverbs 22:6

———————————————

———————————————
Teacher's Signature

Outstanding Achievement

Award

Presented to:

for
Exceptional Work in
Memorizing Catechism Questions 43-60
During the Week of

_____

Train up a child in the way he should go, and when he is old, he will not depart from it.
Proverbs 22:6

_____
Teacher's Signature

Outstanding Achievement

Award

Presented to:

for
Exceptional Work in

_____

During the Week of

_____

Train up a child in the way he should go, and when he is old, he will not depart from it.
Proverbs 22:6

_____
Teacher's Signature